S0-AAF-094

**Ikebana Simplified**

by the same author   *Ikebana*

# Ikebana Simplified

A pictorial introduction to Japanese Flower arrangement

by Georgie Davidson

with line illustrations by Lindsay Pope

Arthur Barker Limited   5 Winsley Street   London W 1

SBN 213 17615 7

*Printed in Great Britain by Lowe & Brydone (Printers) Ltd., London*

# CONTENTS

# INTRODUCTION

The history of Ikebana – the Japanese Art of Flower Arrangement – can be traced in tapestries and paintings back to the 6th century. Legend has it that the first knowledge of Ikebana was brought to Japan from China by a Prince who had been there to study the famous Chinese arts and crafts. The Prince on his return to Japan built a temple by a lake and a flower master was appointed. Students came to be taught by 'the monk who lives in a hut by the lake'. The first arrangements were almost certainly floral offerings to Buddha. These simple placings in the temple became very stylised and elaborate and were called *Rikkwa*. They usually comprised a central pine branch, round which were placed groups of different materials. (To the right, to the left, to the front, to the lower right, to the left rear, to the right front, to the lower front and at the base.) The groups were arranged in three styles: the *Shin* (upright – shown here) style, usually in tall bronze containers; the *Gyo* (low) style of great width in deep rectangular containers; and the *So* (hanging) style in a boat shaped suspended container. The *Rikkwa* arrangements, being formal and elaborate, were chiefly made by priests and noblemen. To accord with the *Chanoyu*—the tea ceremony—which was being taught more widely and was becoming increasingly important in the lives of the people, a simple flower arrangement was needed. The *Nageire* (thrown-in) style was created. This was also called *Chabana* and accepted as being suitable for the austere setting of the tea ceremony. For this ceremony one or two kinds of flowers were arranged naturally 'as if growing'. Simple, light coloured flowers

*A Lake*                    *Temple*                    *Rikkwa*

were considered appropriate – sometimes a single flower in a slender vase. The state of mind of the arranger was considered most important.

The ceremony took place in the tea house – a room of basically simple proportions and devoid of ornamentation, separated from the main dwelling by a garden. Its sole use and purpose was for the *Chanoyu*, and the spiritual joy experienced through simplicity. The extreme formality of *Rikkwa* and the simplicity of the *Nageire-Chabana* were eventually combined and the *Shoka-Seikwa* style envolved. This was less formal than the *Rikkwa* but more complex than the *Chabana*. Both Man and Earth aspire to greater things and so the flowers or branches representing them are always placed with their tips looking towards Heaven. A balance must be achieved between the male and the female, the light and the dark, sunshine and shadow, the positive and the negative aspects of the materials. The principle of the three main lines in the arrangement, symbolising Heaven, Man and Earth, was universally adopted. Even numbers of lines, flowers or branches were rarely used, for they tend to produce symmetry and even balance which gives an impression of lifelessness. So a change came about and flower arrangements which had previously been religious offerings were made for human appreciation, and Ikebana, as now known, began to develop and to be accepted as an art. In the Japanese home it became the practice to place an Ikebana arrangement in the *Tokonoma* – a large alcove like recess – previously reserved for treasures.

Up to this point all the flowers and branches had been kept in position either

*Shoka*                     *Tea House*                     *Chabana*

by bunches of reed or bamboo stems tied together, or by pieces of wood split and wedged into the neck of the container. Later, when shallow dishes were introduced, this was impracticable and Shippos made of lead moulded into various shapes – crabs, dragons, honeycombs – were used to hold the stems in the desired position. The next development was the *Moribana* 'piled up flowers' style, an adaptation of the baskets of 'piled up petals' used in the temples. The principle of three was still the basis of the designs, which are laid down by individual schools. Some place Heaven – the longest line – in a vertical position, some in a slanting position, some move it about. The choice of materials is now left to the arranger except for special festivals. For boys – irises; for girls – peach; for moon viewing – pampas grass; for New Year – pine, bamboo and plum. Most plants can be used, if one so desires, to convey messages. Pine, because of its resilience and strength signifies long life; plum, courage – since it is the first to brave the winter and bloom; lotus, purity – its blooms rising unsullied through the mud. Some colour combinations are considered good and some not. Red and white are used for happy occasions and white for sad ones. The twentieth century and the *Moribana* style have produced the *Kenzan* (mountain of needles) known in the West as a pinholder. Its use greatly simplifies arranging.

One of the basic values of this form of art is its ability to convey spiritual enlightenment through the handling and use of flowers and natural materials. The tranquility thus enjoyed enables a person to create an arrangement which is

*Tokanoma*                     *Nageire*                     *Moribana*

essentially an extension of their personality. Modern trends have, of course, made an impact on Ikebana and have adjusted it to twentieth century concepts of art. These forms are achieved by using flowers and other natural materials for colour, texture and line, but in an unnatural way. Beyond this is the abstract form, a term which is self-explanatory. It is, I think, in these later stages, that the early teachings of Ikebana are invaluable. In this book I have tried to present a number of designs in cartoon form. It is not possible for most of us to spend a vast sum of money visiting Japan or to study as much as we would like to. However, given a pattern, it should be possible for us to achieve a reasonably commendable arrangement in the Eastern style. But unless you go beyond this and can draw from the Art some tranquility and strength you will be the poorer and I shall have failed in the object of this book. Appreciation is important but spiritual enlightenment is the ultimate aim. The concepts to remember when following these cartoons are that Heaven is the most important line, Earth is the base, and that Man is the intermediate, the reconciling, line.

*Classical*                    *Modern*                    *Abstract*

# KEY AND MEASUREMENTS

Key

● ⬤ LONGEST LINE ~ HEAVEN. SUPPLEMENTARY TO ●.

■ ▪ INTERMEDIATE LINE MAN. SUPPLEMENTARY TO ■.

▲ ▲ SHORTEST LINE ~ EARTH. SUPPLEMENTARY TO ▲.

T OAR ~ BOAT ARRANGEMENTS ONLY.

Measurements

'D' DIAMETER OF CONTAINER.

'L' LENGTH OF CONTAINER.

'H' HEIGHT OF CONTAINER.

# INDEX OF FLOWERS

# SPRING

THE CONTAINERS TRADITIONALLY USED FOR SPRING ARRANGEMENTS
ARE CERAMIC OR OF GLASS. SHOULD YOU HOWEVER WISH TO USE A
METAL ONE, WHICH YET HAS THE DEWY LOOK OF SPRING, CHILL
IT THOROUGHLY AND THEN SPRAY IT WITH AN ATOMISER.

WEIGHTY BRANCHES OF BLOSSOM WILL NEED THE STRENGTH
OF THE "VERTICAL AND HORIZONTAL" OR "SINGLE BAR" FIXING CALLED
A KUBARI.

CUT THE HORIZONTAL STICKS ~ PINE, DOGWOOD OR FINE
GRAINED WOOD ~ TO THE OUTSIDE MEASUREMENT OF THE CONTAINER
AND THEN TRIM IT CAREFULLY UNTIL IT FITS.

DON'T USE FORCE OR YOU WILL BREAK THE CONTAINER.

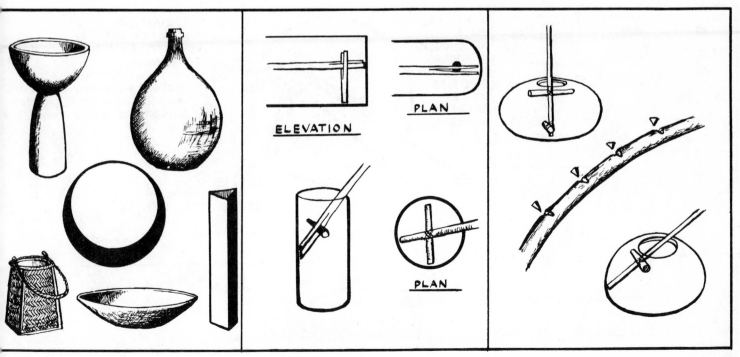

ELEVATION

PLAN

PLAN

## A Natural Style

BLOSSOMING BRANCHES PLACED AT ANGLES OF 45°, 15°, AND 75° RESPECTIVELY FROM THE VERTICAL, ARE USED FOR THIS SPRING ARRANGEMENT.

THE SUPPLEMENTARY LINES ARE EITHER TULIPS OR BRANCHES.

IN SUMMER THE SPRING BLOSSOMS MAY BE REPLACED BY FOLIAGE AND SUMMER FLOWERS.

SOME BENDING OF THE BRANCHES WILL BE NECESSARY

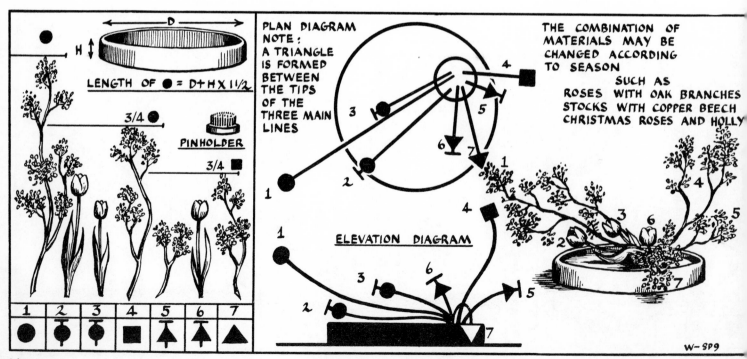

LENGTH OF ● = D+H X 1½

3/4 ●

PINHOLDER

3/4 ■

PLAN DIAGRAM
NOTE:
A TRIANGLE IS FORMED BETWEEN THE TIPS OF THE THREE MAIN LINES

ELEVATION DIAGRAM

THE COMBINATION OF MATERIALS MAY BE CHANGED ACCORDING TO SEASON
SUCH AS
ROSES WITH OAK BRANCHES
STOCKS WITH COPPER BEECH
CHRISTMAS ROSES AND HOLLY

W-SP9

## Classical Style

● A BUD TURNED TO THE LEFT AT AN ANGLE OF 45°.

■ A BUD TURNED TO THE RIGHT AT AN ANGLE OF 45°.

⊞'s FULL FLOWERS PLACED ON THE OUTSIDE OF ● AND ■ AND TURNED SLIGHTLY ASKEW.

▲ SHORTEST FLOWER PLACED INSIDE OF ● AND TURNING DIFFERENTLY. ALLOW THE FLOWERS TO 'CHATTER'.

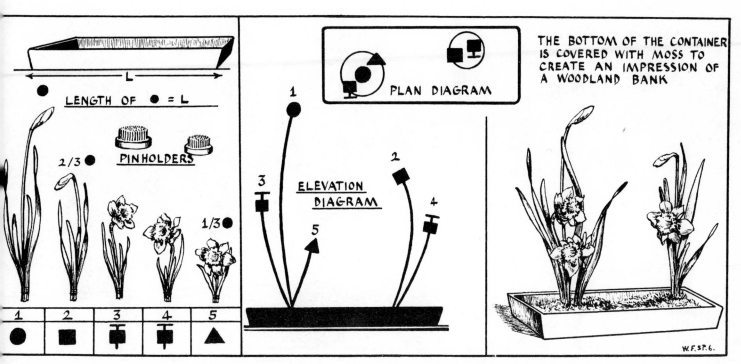

LENGTH OF ● = L

2/3 ●

PINHOLDERS

1/3 ●

| 1 | 2 | 3 | 4 | 5 |
|---|---|---|---|---|
| ● | ■ | ⊞ | ⊞ | ▲ |

PLAN DIAGRAM

ELEVATION DIAGRAM

THE BOTTOM OF THE CONTAINER IS COVERED WITH MOSS TO CREATE AN IMPRESSION OF A WOODLAND BANK

W.F.SP.6.

15

# A Free Style

● FORSYTHIA BRANCHES  ■ FORSYTHIA BRANCHES
■ TULIPS , ■ TULIPS

IT IS THE NATURE OF THE FORSYTHIA SHRUB TO
BRANCH AND CURVE GRACEFULLY BUT IF IT IS NOT
POSSIBLE FOR YOU TO FIND ONE BRANCH WITH THE
DESIRED LATERALS, ADD ANOTHER ONE.

THE ESSENCE OF THIS ARRANGEMENT IS TO PRESENT
MOVEMENT AND ABUNDANCE OF SPRING. TULIP LEAVES
ARE ESSENTIAL TO COVER THE BASES OF THE BRANCHES
ADD THESE IF TULIP DOES NOT HAVE THEM IN THE
RIGHT PLACE.

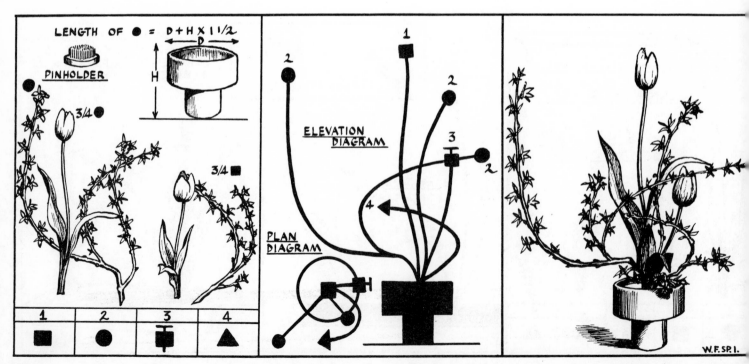

LENGTH OF ● = D + H × 1 1/2

PINHOLDER

3/4 ●

3/4 ■

| 1 | 2 | 3 | 4 |
|---|---|---|---|
| ■ | ● | ⊤ | ▲ |

ELEVATION DIAGRAM

PLAN DIAGRAM

W.F. SP.I.

## A Classical Style

A BOAT SAILING TO THE RIGHT IS DEEMED TO BE HOMEWARD BOUND.

●, ■, T, WILLOW, JUST SHOWING ITS NEW LEAF.

▲, ⊼,    IRIS

THE OAR, A PECULIARITY OF THE BOAT ARRANGEMENTS SHOULD BE SUFFICIENTLY RAISED TO AVOID TOUCHING THE SURFACE.

IT REPRESENTS THE WAKE

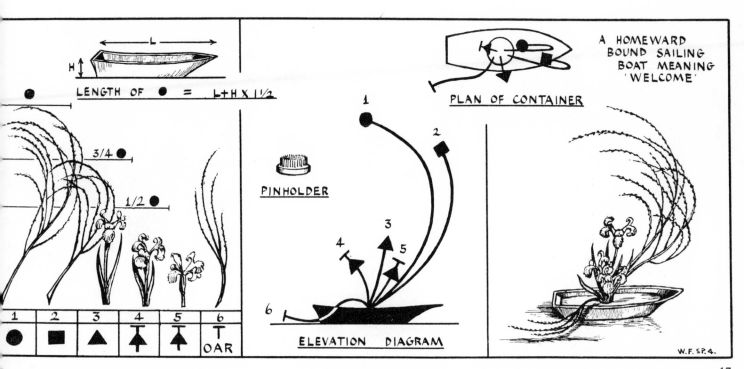

LENGTH OF ● = L+H X 1½

3/4 ●

1/2 ●

PINHOLDER

PLAN OF CONTAINER

A HOMEWARD BOUND SAILING BOAT MEANING 'WELCOME'

ELEVATION DIAGRAM

| 1 | 2 | 3 | 4 | 5 | 6 |
|---|---|---|---|---|---|
| ● | ■ | ▲ | ⊼ | ⊼ | T OAR |

W.F. SP. 4.

# A Classical Style

TAKE 3 TULIPS AND 4 LEAVES. PLACE THEM AS THOUGH GROWING, SUPPORTING EACH FLOWER WITH LEAVES.

SINCE THE LEAVES FORM THE MAJOR PART OF THE DESIGN, IT WILL NOT BE SPOILT IF THE TULIPS 'WALK AROUND'.

BE CAREFUL THAT YOU DO NOT ALLOW THE ▲ LEAF TO HANG.

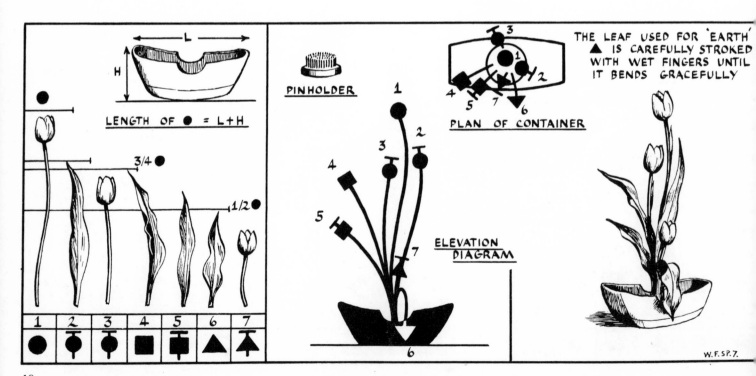

LENGTH OF ● = L+H

3/4 ●

1/2 ●

| 1 | 2 | 3 | 4 | 5 | 6 | 7 |
|---|---|---|---|---|---|---|
| ● | ● | ● | ■ | ■ | ▲ | ▲ |

PINHOLDER

PLAN OF CONTAINER

ELEVATION DIAGRAM

THE LEAF USED FOR 'EARTH' ▲ IS CAREFULLY STROKED WITH WET FINGERS UNTIL IT BENDS GRACEFULLY

W.F. SP. 7.

18

## A Natural Style

PRUNUS TRILOBA

GARDENIA LEAVES AND FLOWERS

THE GARDENIAS HAVE SHORT STEMS.
THE PRUNUS OBTAINABLE IN FLOWER
SHOPS IN THE SPRING IS GENERALLY
STRAIGHT.

I HAVE EMPHASIZED BOTH CHARACTERISTICS
IN THIS DESIGN AND, TO RETURN THE EYE
TO THE CENTRE, HAVE CRACKED (NOT BROKEN)
ONE STEM

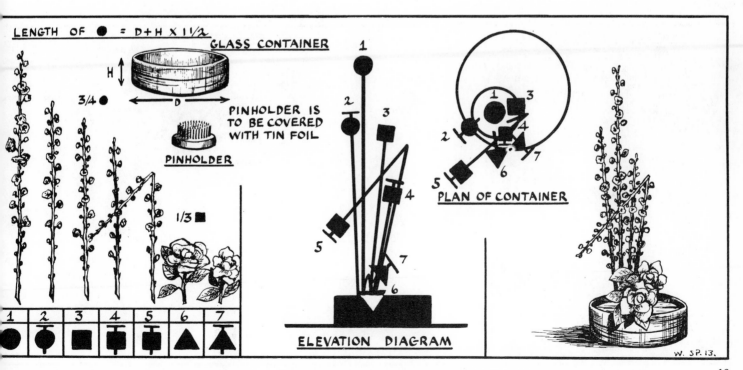

LENGTH OF ● = D+H X 1½

GLASS CONTAINER

PINHOLDER IS TO BE COVERED WITH TIN FOIL

PINHOLDER

PLAN OF CONTAINER

ELEVATION DIAGRAM

W. SP. 13.

## A Natural Style

●, ▲, YELLOW LILIES, ☨ CUPRESSUS

THE PINHOLDER IS PLACED AT THE RIGHT FRONT OF THE CONTAINER AND THE LILIES TO LOOK DIAGONALLY, ONE TO THE RIGHT AND ONE TO THE LEFT.

AT THE BASE OF ▲ IS A MATERIAL CONTRASTING IN TEXTURE.

I HAVE USED A BLACK AND WHITE STRIPED CONTAINER FOR CONTRAST OF COLOUR.

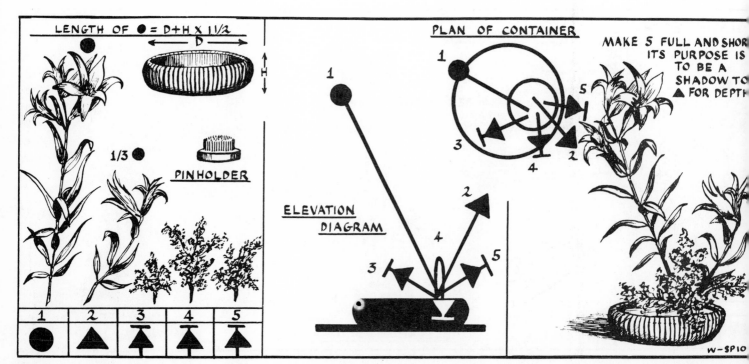

LENGTH OF ● = D+H X 1½

1/3 ●

PINHOLDER

| 1 | 2 | 3 | 4 | 5 |
|---|---|---|---|---|

PLAN OF CONTAINER

ELEVATION DIAGRAM

MAKE 5 FULL AND SHORT ITS PURPOSE IS TO BE A SHADOW TO ▲ FOR DEPTH

W-SP10

## A Modern Style

**●, ■, ▲, JONQUILS**

THIS IS A USEFUL ARRANGEMENT TO MAKE WHEN JONQUILS ARE CHEAP AND SOLD WITHOUT THEIR LEAVES.

MAKE A RING OF "FACES" FOR ● AND TIE LOOSELY AT THE NECK. PLACE ANOTHER RING AROUND ● THREE QUARTERS OF THE WAY UP FOR ■ AND TIE SIMILARLY.

TIE AGAIN AT THE BASE AND PLACE ON THE CENTRE OF THE PINHOLDER.

SURROUND THIS WITH THE REMAINDER OF THE FLOWERS FOR ▲.

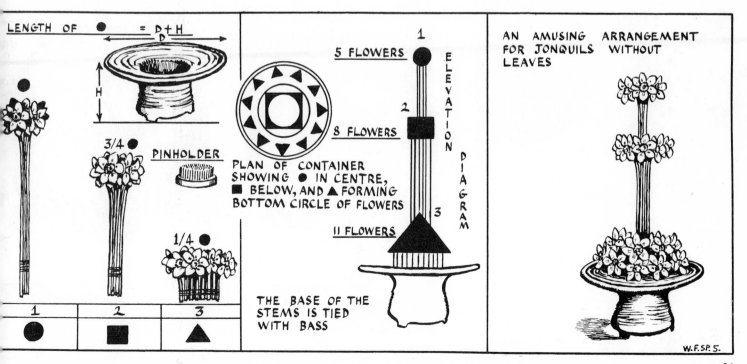

LENGTH OF ● = D + H

H

3/4 ●

PINHOLDER

1/4 ●

| 1 | 2 | 3 |
|---|---|---|
| ● | ■ | ▲ |

5 FLOWERS

8 FLOWERS

11 FLOWERS

PLAN OF CONTAINER SHOWING ● IN CENTRE, ■ BELOW, AND ▲ FORMING BOTTOM CIRCLE OF FLOWERS

ELEVATION DIAGRAM

THE BASE OF THE STEMS IS TIED WITH BASS

AN AMUSING ARRANGEMENT FOR JONQUILS WITHOUT LEAVES

W.F.SP.5.

# A Classical Style

●, ■, VIBURNUM FRAGRANS, ▲ FREESIA.

THE MOON WAXES AND WANES. HIGH TO THE LEFT WAXING — LOW TO THE RIGHT WANING.

VIBURNUM FRAGRANS WITH ITS EARLY SPRING GROWTH IS A PERFECT BRANCH MATERIAL. COMBINE IT WITH THE SMOOTH CREAMINESS OF DOUBLE YELLOW FREESIAS.

THE MOON MAY STAND ON A TABLE OR BE SUSPENDED.

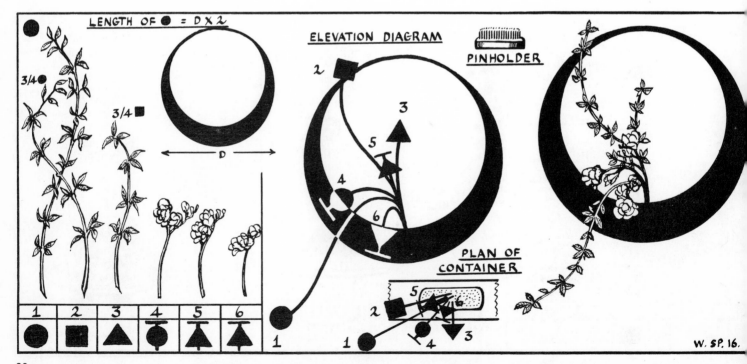

W. SP. 16.

# A Natural Style

MAHONIA AND YELLOW CALLA LILIES

●, ⬛̄, ⬛, MAHONIA BRANCHES
▲, ▲s, YELLOW LILIES.

THE COMBINATION OF THIS PARTICULAR
MAHONIA WITH YELLOW FLOWERS NEVER
FAILS TO PLEASE. ~ THE BRANCHES ARE
PLACED IN A SLANTING POSITION THE BETTER
TO APPRECIATE THEIR LEAVES. ~ POLISH
THE LEAVES WITH MILK OR GLYCERINE AFTER
TRIMMING.
BIND THE LILY STEMS AT THE
BASE TO STOP THEM FROM CURLING.

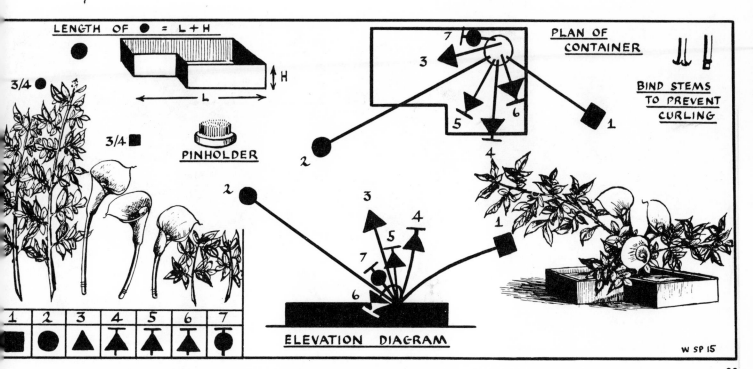

LENGTH OF ● = L + H

3/4 ●

3/4 ⬛

PINHOLDER

PLAN OF CONTAINER

BIND STEMS TO PREVENT CURLING

ELEVATION DIAGRAM

W SP 15

| 1 | 2 | 3 | 4 | 5 | 6 | 7 |
|---|---|---|---|---|---|---|
| ⬛ | ● | ▲ | ▲ | ▲ | ▲ | ⬤ |

# A Classical Style

●, ■, ▲, BROOM ~ ●, ■, ▲, TULIPS

A NAVY BLUE CONTAINER, WHITE FLOWERING BROOM AND RED ALADDIN TULIPS IN TWO CLASSICAL ARRANGEMENTS IN ONE CONTAINER.

THE SECOND ● IS THREE QUARTERS THE LENGTH OF THE FIRST, WITH ■ AND ▲ CORRESPONDINGLY SHORTER.

SMALL STONES SCATTERED AROUND THE PINHOLDERS TO CONCEAL THEM.

LENGTH OF 1st ● = L + H × 1½

H

L

PINHOLDERS

2/3 ●

1/2 ●

| 1 | 2 | 3 | 4 | 5 |
|---|---|---|---|---|
| ● | ● | ■ | ■ | ▲ |

PLAN OF CONTAINER

THE TULIPS IN EACH CASE ARE 3/4 THE LENGTH OF THEIR COUNTERPARTS IN BROOM

ELEVATION DIAGRAM

W. SP. 18.

# SUMMER

BASKET AND BAMBOO TRAYS ARE POPULAR AND SEASONABLE FOR SUMMER USE. BE CAREFUL TO CHECK THAT LINERS OF BAMBOO ARE WATERTIGHT AFTER WINTER STORAGE. IN THE FLAT TRAY A WELL PINHOLDER WOULD BE USED.

THE NEW SPRING GROWTH REQUIRES GENTLE BENDING, STEADY PRESSURE OVER THE THUMBS ( AS ILLUSTRATED) IS GENERALLY ENOUGH.

FOR THE ACUTE ANGLES USE THE "DIAGONAL CUT" METHOD. ON THE UNDERSIDE OF THE BRANCH CUT, AT AN ANGLE OF 45°, THE BRANCH APPROXIMATELY 1/3 WAY THROUGH, PLACE THE FOREFINGER AND THUMB ON EITHER SIDE OF THIS AND TWIST AND BEND ~

THIS TECHNIQUE IS PARTICULARLY USEFUL FOR THE OAR IN THE BOAT ARRANGEMENTS.

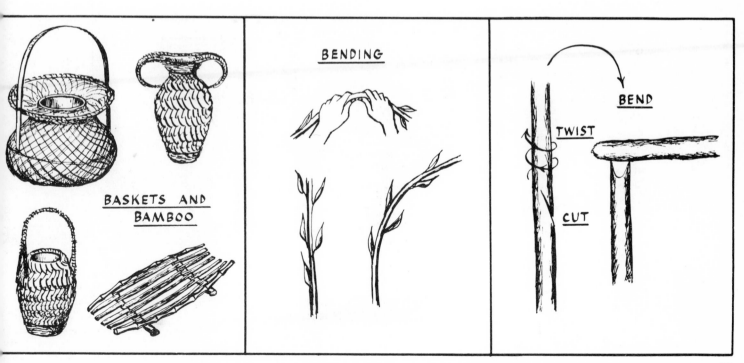

BASKETS AND BAMBOO

BENDING

TWIST

BEND

CUT

# A Classical Style

●, ■, ▲, DELPHINIUMS

DELPHINIUMS OF VARIOUS SHADES OF BLUE, OR LUPINS, OENOTHERA OR ANY SUCH FLOWERS CAN BE USED FOR THIS 'BOAT AT ANCHOR'

NOTE THAT THE UNDERDEVELOPED TIP IS CUT ENTIRELY FROM ▲ AND SHORTENED ON ■. THIS IS THE ONLY ONE OF THE BOAT ARRANGEMENTS WHICH IS PLACED ON A BASE.

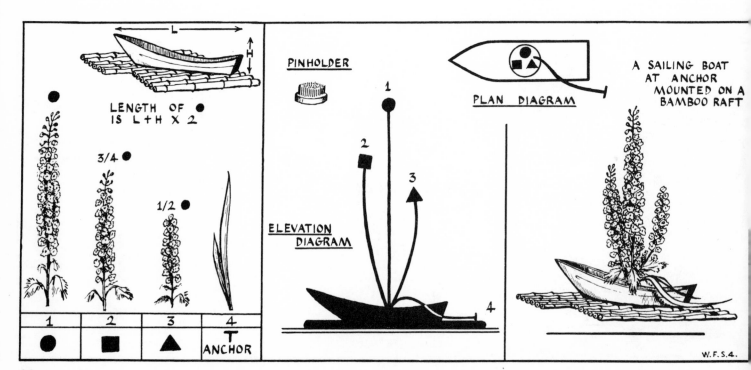

L

H

LENGTH OF ● IS L + H X 2

● 

3/4 ●

1/2 ●

| 1 | 2 | 3 | 4 |
|---|---|---|---|
| ● | ■ | ▲ | T ANCHOR |

PINHOLDER

ELEVATION DIAGRAM

1

2

3

4

PLAN DIAGRAM

A SAILING BOAT AT ANCHOR MOUNTED ON A BAMBOO RAFT

W.F.S.4.

26

# A Natural Style

●, ■, SMALL BULRUSHES STRIPPED OF LEAVES.

▲ PEONY FLOWER, ⟁ LEAVES.

AN ARRANGEMENT WHICH SHOWS TO ITS FULL MAGNIFICENCE THE FLOWER OF THE PEONY AND ITS LEAVES.

AN ALTERNATIVE MATERIAL FOR THE BACKGROUND COULD BE REEDS, OR GRASSES.

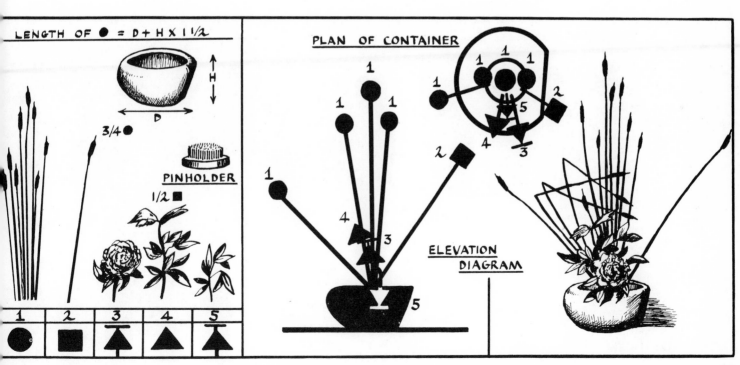

LENGTH OF ● = D + H X 1½

3/4 ●

PINHOLDER

1/2 ■

PLAN OF CONTAINER

ELEVATION DIAGRAM

| 1 | 2 | 3 | 4 | 5 |
|---|---|---|---|---|

## A Free Style

AN ANTIQUE BOTTLE, A TWIST OF
DRIED STRIPPED WOOD, TWO HYDRANGEA
FLOWERS AND A FEW LEAVES.

REMOVE ALL LEAVES BELOW THE WATER
LINE AND SHORTEN STEMS TO 2 INCHES
SO THAT THEY ARE NOT SEEN.

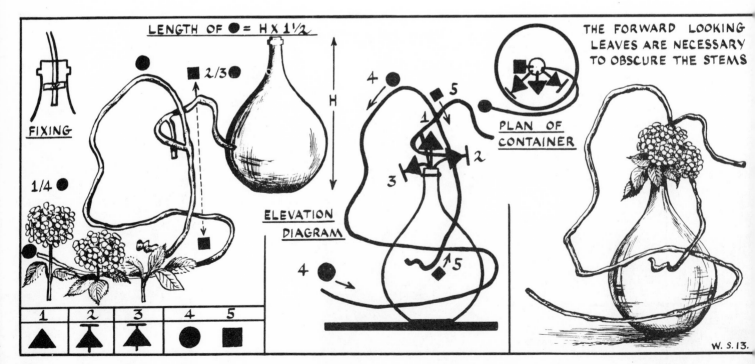

# A Classical Style

FIVE ROSES WITH CAREFULLY POLISHED AND TRIMMED LEAVES ARE GROUPED AS THOUGH GROWING FROM ONE POINT IN THE CENTRE OF THE CONTAINER.

THE PINHOLDER IS CONCEALED WITH SMALL STONES.

IT IS IMPORTANT FOR BALANCE THAT TIP OF ● RETURNS TO A POINT OVER ITS BASE.

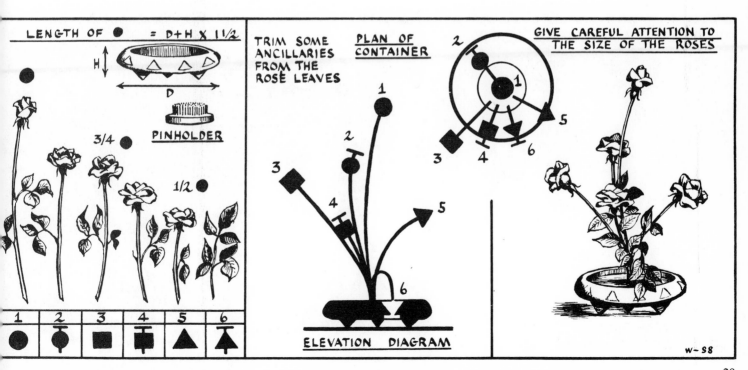

LENGTH OF ● = D + H X 1½

H

D

PINHOLDER

3/4

1/2

| 1 | 2 | 3 | 4 | 5 | 6 |
|---|---|---|---|---|---|

TRIM SOME ANCILLARIES FROM THE ROSE LEAVES

PLAN OF CONTAINER

GIVE CAREFUL ATTENTION TO THE SIZE OF THE ROSES

ELEVATION DIAGRAM

W-58

29

# A Natural Style

●, ▲, ANTHURIUMS ～ ◐, ▲, CALADIUM LEAVES
EXOTIC MATERIALS ARE EXPENSIVE BUT
PARADOXICALLY THE ANTHURIUM IF BOUGHT
WHEN FRESH, MAKES AN ECONOMICAL
ARRANGEMENT BECAUSE OF ITS LASTING
QUALITIES.

SUBSTITUTES FOR THE CALADIUM
LEAVES COULD BE THOSE OF THE ANTHURIUM
OR BEGONIA PLANTS.

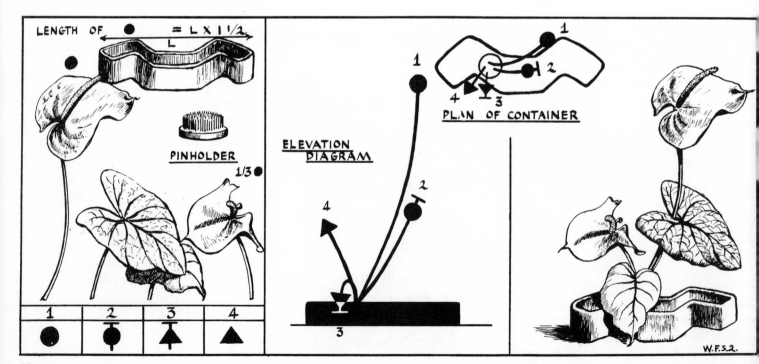

# A Modern Style

●, ■, PRIVET ~ ▲, MARIGOLDS

GROUP SINGLE STEMS OF PRIVET STRIPPED OF MOST OF ITS LEAVES FOR ● AND ■, AND BEND.

ADD BRIGHT MARIGOLDS AND AN AMUSING CONTAINER AND YOU HAVE A BRIGHT LONG LASTING MODERN ARRANGEMENT.

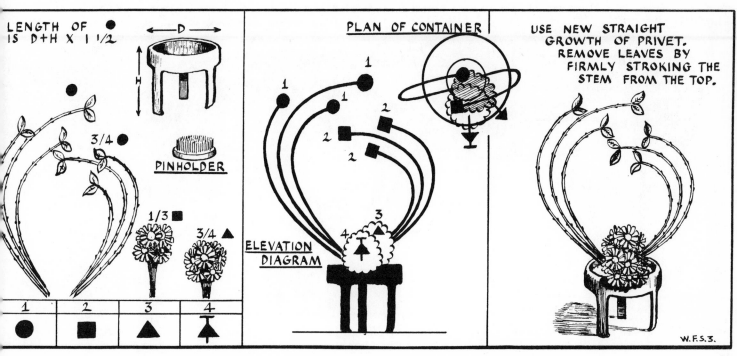

LENGTH OF ●
IS D+H X 1 ½

D

H

3/4 ●

PINHOLDER

1/3 ■

3/4 ▲

| 1 | 2 | 3 | 4 |
|---|---|---|---|
| ● | ■ | ▲ | ▲ |

PLAN OF CONTAINER

1
1
1
2
2
2
3
4

ELEVATION DIAGRAM

USE NEW STRAIGHT GROWTH OF PRIVET. REMOVE LEAVES BY FIRMLY STROKING THE STEM FROM THE TOP.

W.F.S.3.

31

## A Classical Style

●, ▲, AMARYLLIS ∼ ⬤, ■, ⬥s, LEAVES. FLOWERS WITH LONG BARE STEMS ARE USUALLY AMENABLE TO THE CLASSICAL STYLE OF ARRANGING.

THE AMARYLLIS IS NO EXCEPTION. AS ONE CAN RARELY BUY THE LEAVES WITH THE FLOWERS, SUBSTITUTE THOSE OF CLIVIA, IRIS, GLADIOLI, OR ANY SIMILAR SHAPED LEAF.

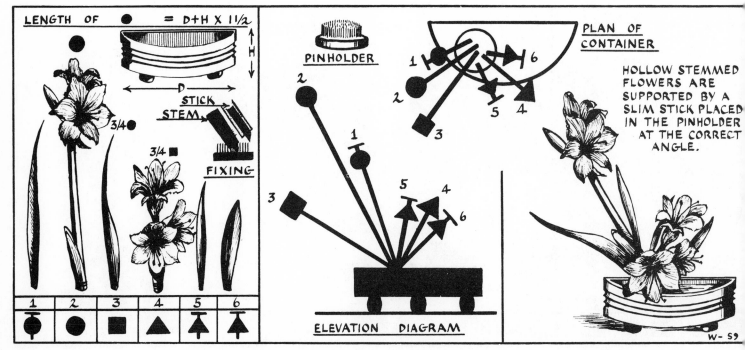

LENGTH OF ● = D+H X 1½

3/4 ●

3/4 ■

STICK STEM

FIXING

| 1 | 2 | 3 | 4 | 5 | 6 |
|---|---|---|---|---|---|
| ⬤ | ● | ■ | ▲ | ⬥ | ⬥ |

PINHOLDER

PLAN OF CONTAINER

HOLLOW STEMMED FLOWERS ARE SUPPORTED BY A SLIM STICK PLACED IN THE PINHOLDER AT THE CORRECT ANGLE.

ELEVATION DIAGRAM

W-59

# A Natural Style

THESE TWO TYPES OF FLOWERS HAVE LONG BEEN A POPULAR COMBINATION BOTH HAVE A SUPERB COLOUR RANGE.

THE STRAIGHT LINES OF THE GLADIOLI ARE ENHANCED BY THE CURVES OF THE GERBERA.

GERBERAS SHOULD BE ARRANGED IN SHALLOW WATER.

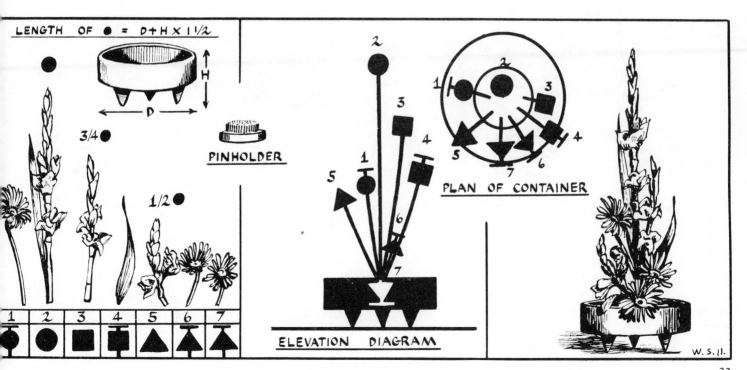

LENGTH OF ● = D + H × 1½

3/4 ●

1/2 ●

PINHOLDER

| 1 | 2 | 3 | 4 | 5 | 6 | 7 |

PLAN OF CONTAINER

ELEVATION DIAGRAM

W.S.II.

# A Natural Style

●, ■, AGAPANTHUS, ⚘, ▲, ⊼ ROSES, ⬛ LEAVES.
BLUE AGAPANTHUS AND WHITE ROSES
IN A BLUE CONTAINER.
    SUPPORT THESE WITH GREEN
LEAVES OF THE IRIS, GLADIOLUS OR
BETTER STILL, IF AVAILABLE, THE
LEAVES OF THE AGAPANTHUS ITSELF.

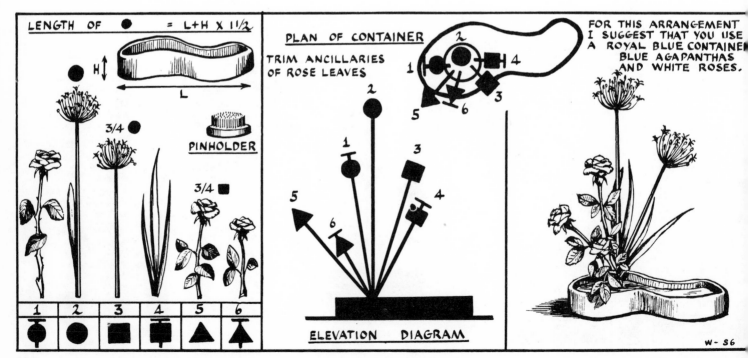

LENGTH OF ● = L+H X 1½

PINHOLDER

3/4 ●

3/4 ■

| 1 | 2 | 3 | 4 | 5 | 6 |
|---|---|---|---|---|---|

PLAN OF CONTAINER

TRIM ANCILLARIES
OF ROSE LEAVES

ELEVATION DIAGRAM

FOR THIS ARRANGEMENT
I SUGGEST THAT YOU USE
A ROYAL BLUE CONTAINER
BLUE AGAPANTHAS
AND WHITE ROSES.

W-56

# A Natural Style

A MORIMONO IS AN ARRANGEMENT IN WHICH FRUIT OR VEGETABLES DOMINATE. I HAVE USED PEACHES AND ORCHIDS. BY PLACING THESE AT DIFFERENT ANGLES ONE BREAKS THE 'PAIR'.

WRAP THE ENDS OF THE FLOWER STEMS WITH DAMP COTTON WOOL AND COVER WITH OILED SILK OR FOIL.

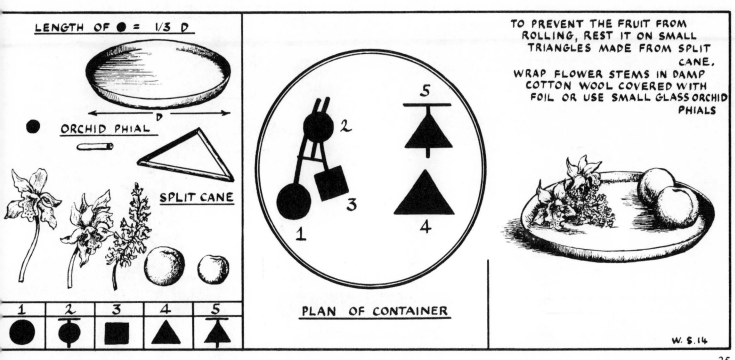

LENGTH OF ● = 1/3 D

ORCHID PHIAL

SPLIT CANE

| 1 | 2 | 3 | 4 | 5 |
|---|---|---|---|---|
| ● | ● | ■ | ▲ | ▲ |

PLAN OF CONTAINER

TO PREVENT THE FRUIT FROM ROLLING, REST IT ON SMALL TRIANGLES MADE FROM SPLIT CANE.
WRAP FLOWER STEMS IN DAMP COTTON WOOL COVERED WITH FOIL OR USE SMALL GLASS ORCHID PHIALS

W. S. 14

## A Free Style

● STRONG UPRIGHT GLADIOLUS BUDS AND LEAVES.
▲ THE FULL BLOOMS ARE ARRANGED
   IN A SOLID BLOCK OF COLOUR.
■ SWIRLS OF BLEACHED BAMBOO.

THE GLADIOLI MAY BE REPLACED BY ANY TALL
STRAIGHT FLOWERS AND THE BAMBOO BY ARCHING
SPRAYS OF BLOSSOM ~ BRIDAL WREATH SPIRAEA ~,
EUPHORBIA OR CHERRY.

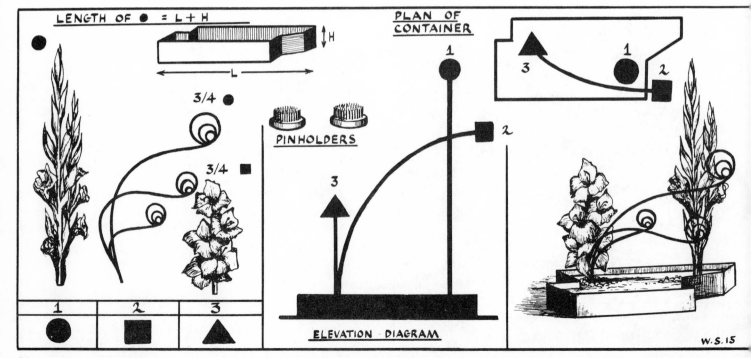

LENGTH OF ● = L + H

3/4 ●

3/4 ■

PINHOLDERS

PLAN OF CONTAINER

| 1 | 2 | 3 |
|---|---|---|
| ● | ■ | ▲ |

ELEVATION · DIAGRAM

W.S. 15

# AUTUMN

BE CAREFUL TO CHOOSE CONTAINERS AT THIS TIME OF YEAR
THAT WILL HARMONISE WITH THE AUTUMNAL COLOURS OF THE
BERRIES AND FOLIAGE.

LESS WATER WILL BE SHOWN THAN IN SUMMER OR
SPRING. WOOD USED AT THE BASE OF AN ARRANGEMENT IS BETTER
IF WATERPROOFED.

WHEN CHOOSING PINHOLDERS MAKE CERTAIN THAT THEY
ARE SUFFICIENTLY HEAVY FOR THE JOB AND THAT THEY HAVE FIRM,
STRONG AND RUSTPROOF PINS.

THE LEAD SNAKE IS A USEFUL FIXING FOR FLOWERS IN
GLASS CONTAINERS. DO NOT ALLOW THE STEMS TO PROTRUDE BELOW
THE FIXING AND SO SPOIL THE EFFECT OF CLEAR WATER.

THE TOOL KIT FEATURED ~ SAW, DOUBLE EDGED KNIFE, SMALL
AXE, SHEARS, SYRINGE AND PINHOLDER STRAIGHTENER IS A USEFUL
AND EFFICIENT ADJUNCT.

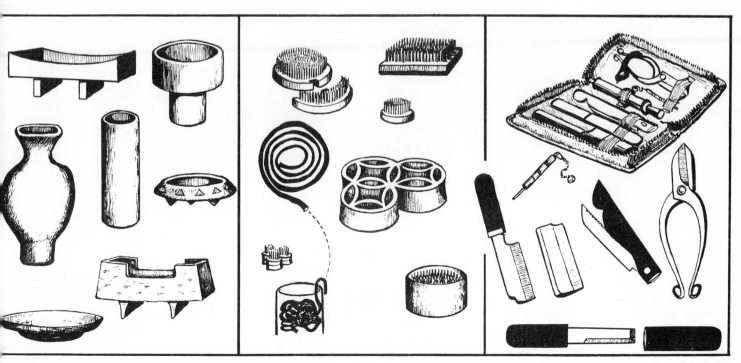

## A Natural Style

● ALDER BRANCH, ■ ▲ CHRYSANTHEMUMS

IN AUTUMN A BARE BRANCH COMBINED
WITH LONG LASTING CHRYSANTHEMUMS
CAN GIVE GREAT PLEASURE.
ONE DOES NOT NORMALLY USE A
BASKET IN AUTUMN.

I HAVE DONE SO ON THIS OCCASION
BECAUSE THE WEAVE SUITED SO WELL
THE TEXTURE OF THE SMALL ALDER CONES.

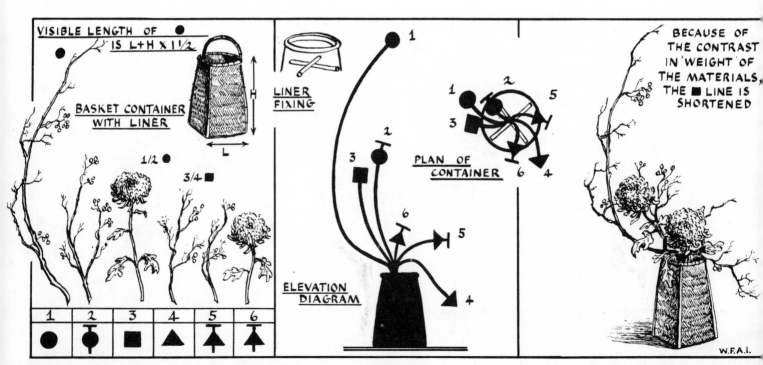

VISIBLE LENGTH OF ●
IS L+H X 1½

BASKET CONTAINER
WITH LINER

1/2 ●
3/4 ■

| 1 | 2 | 3 | 4 | 5 | 6 |
|---|---|---|---|---|---|
| ● | ⬤ | ■ | ▲ | ⟁ | ⟁ |

LINER
FIXING

ELEVATION
DIAGRAM

PLAN OF
CONTAINER

BECAUSE OF
THE CONTRAST
IN WEIGHT OF
THE MATERIALS,
THE ■ LINE IS
SHORTENED

W.F.A.I.

# A Modern Style

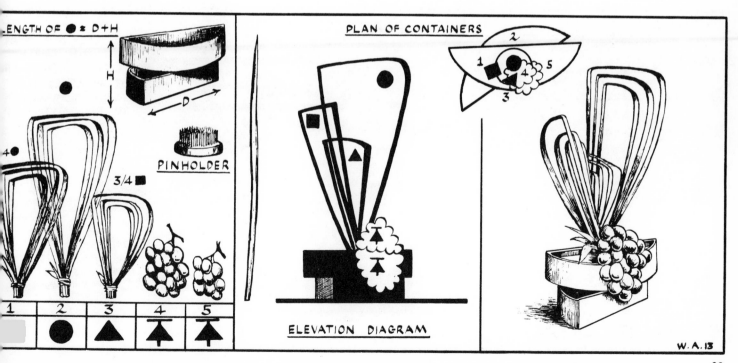

LENGTH OF ● = D+H

PINHOLDER

3/4 ■

| 1 | 2 | 3 | 4 | 5 |
|---|---|---|---|---|
|   | ● | ▲ | ▲ | ▲ |

PLAN OF CONTAINERS

ELEVATION DIAGRAM

W. A. 13

# A Natural Style

SINGLE AND SPRAY CHRYSANTHEMUMS.

●, ⚑, ■, ⊓,    SINGLE ～ ▲, ♠, SPRAY

AFTER PLACING THE MAIN LINES, KEEP TURNING THE CONTAINER TO MAKE CERTAIN THAT ALL FOUR SIDES ARE EQUALLY ATTRACTIVE AND BALANCED.

    THIS ARRANGEMENT IS DESIGNED FOR THE CENTRE OF A TABLE.

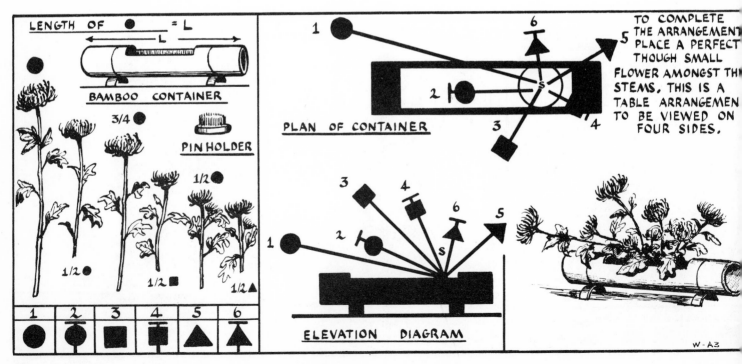

LENGTH OF ● = L

BAMBOO CONTAINER

3/4 ●

PIN HOLDER

1/2 ●

1/2 ●

1/2 ■

1/2 ▲

| 1 | 2 | 3 | 4 | 5 | 6 |
|---|---|---|---|---|---|
| ● | ⚑ | ■ | ⊓ | ▲ | ♠ |

PLAN OF CONTAINER

ELEVATION DIAGRAM

TO COMPLETE THE ARRANGEMENT PLACE A PERFECT THOUGH SMALL FLOWER AMONGST THE STEMS. THIS IS A TABLE ARRANGEMENT TO BE VIEWED ON FOUR SIDES.

W·A3

## Natural Style

●, ■, ▲, PINE ～ ◆, ▼, ▲s, ROSES.

PINE AND ROSES. THREE SHORT ROSES IN A
GROUP. ONE LONG TO SUPPORT ■.
    SMALL PIECES OF PINE ON THE PINHOLDER
AT THE BASE UNITE THE FLOWERS AND BRANCHES.
    THIN THE PINE NEEDLES AS SUGGESTED.
CONCEAL THE CUTS ON THE BRANCHES BY
PAINTING WITH INK OR RUBBING WITH ASH.

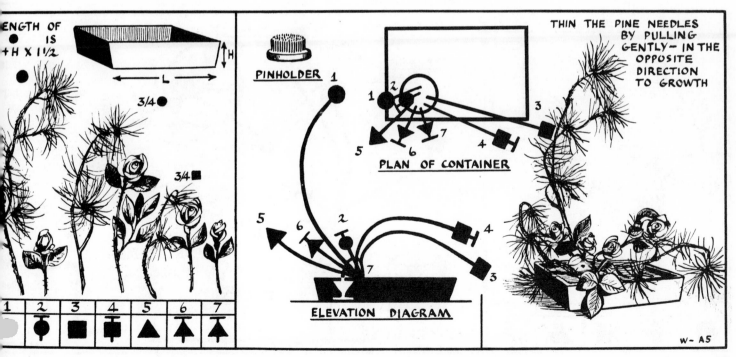

LENGTH OF ● IS +H X 1½

3/4 ●

3/4 ■

PINHOLDER

PLAN OF CONTAINER

ELEVATION DIAGRAM

THIN THE PINE NEEDLES
BY PULLING
GENTLY— IN THE
OPPOSITE
DIRECTION
TO GROWTH

| 1 | 2 | 3 | 4 | 5 | 6 | 7 |
|---|---|---|---|---|---|---|

W- A5

## A Classical Style

●, ◉, ■, GYPSY OAK ~ ▲, ♠, CHRYSANTHEMUMS

GYPSY OAK BRANCHES PRUNED AND
CURVED COMBINED WITH RED SPRAY
CHRYSANTHEMUMS.
THE MATAGI USED NEEDS
PRACTICE IN FIXING.
NEVER USE FORCE OR YOU WILL BREAK
YOUR CONTAINER.
FIRST CUT IT TO THE OUTSIDE MEASUREMENT
OF THE RIM AND THEN WHITTLE AWAY
GRADUALLY. THE TOMEGI, THE TWIG TO
HOLD BRANCHES WHEN PLACED, SHOULD
BE SUPPLE.

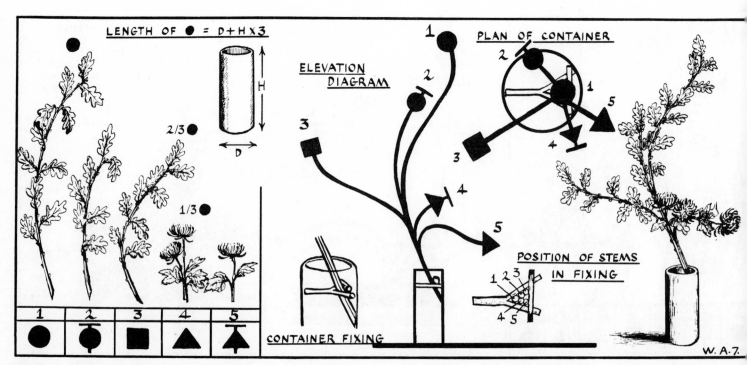

LENGTH OF ● = D+H×3

2/3 ●

1/3 ●

| 1 | 2 | 3 | 4 | 5 |
|---|---|---|---|---|
| ● | ◉ | ■ | ▲ | ♠ |

ELEVATION
DIAGRAM

PLAN OF CONTAINER

POSITION OF STEMS
IN FIXING

CONTAINER FIXING

W. A. 7.

## A Natural Style

AUTUMN BERRIES ~ IN THIS CASE PYRACANTHA ~ AND DRIFT WOOD. BE CAREFUL WITH COLOUR COMBINATIONS OF CONTAINER AND WOOD.

I HAVE USED A DARK ROOT AND A MEDIUM COLOURED STONEWARE CONTAINER WITH AN ASH GLAZE.

BECAUSE OF THE MULTIPLICITY OF BERRIES ON THE BRANCHES, THE ■ LINE IS OMITTED.

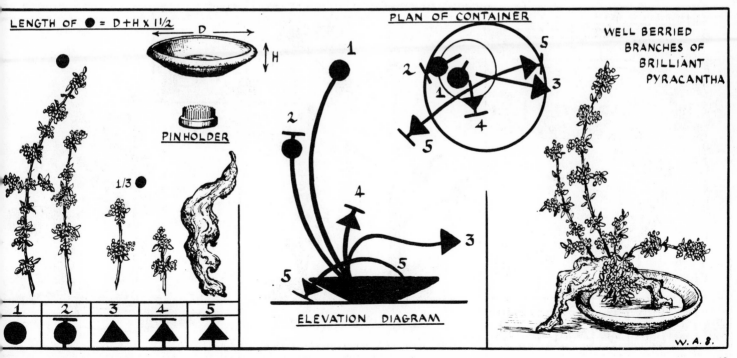

LENGTH OF ● = D + H X 1½

PINHOLDER

PLAN OF CONTAINER

ELEVATION DIAGRAM

WELL BERRIED BRANCHES OF BRILLIANT PYRACANTHA

1/3 ●

| 1 | 2 | 3 | 4 | 5 |

W. A. 8.

# A Natural Style

●, ●, ■, ■, CALLICARPA BERRIES.
▲, ▲, PINK CHRYSANTHEMUMS.

THE NUMBER 8 AND THE TITLE COMBINATION IS GIVEN WHEN TWO COMPLETE ARRANGEMENTS ARE COMBINED IN THE SAME OR SEPARATE CONTAINERS.

I HAVE USED CALLICARPA WITH ITS PURPLE BERRIES IN AN UPRIGHT STYLE FOR THE FIRST, AND PINK CHRYSANTHEMUMS FOR THE SECOND.

COMPLETE BY PLACING A SMALL PIECE OF DRIFTWOOD AT THE BASE OF THE FIRST GROUP.

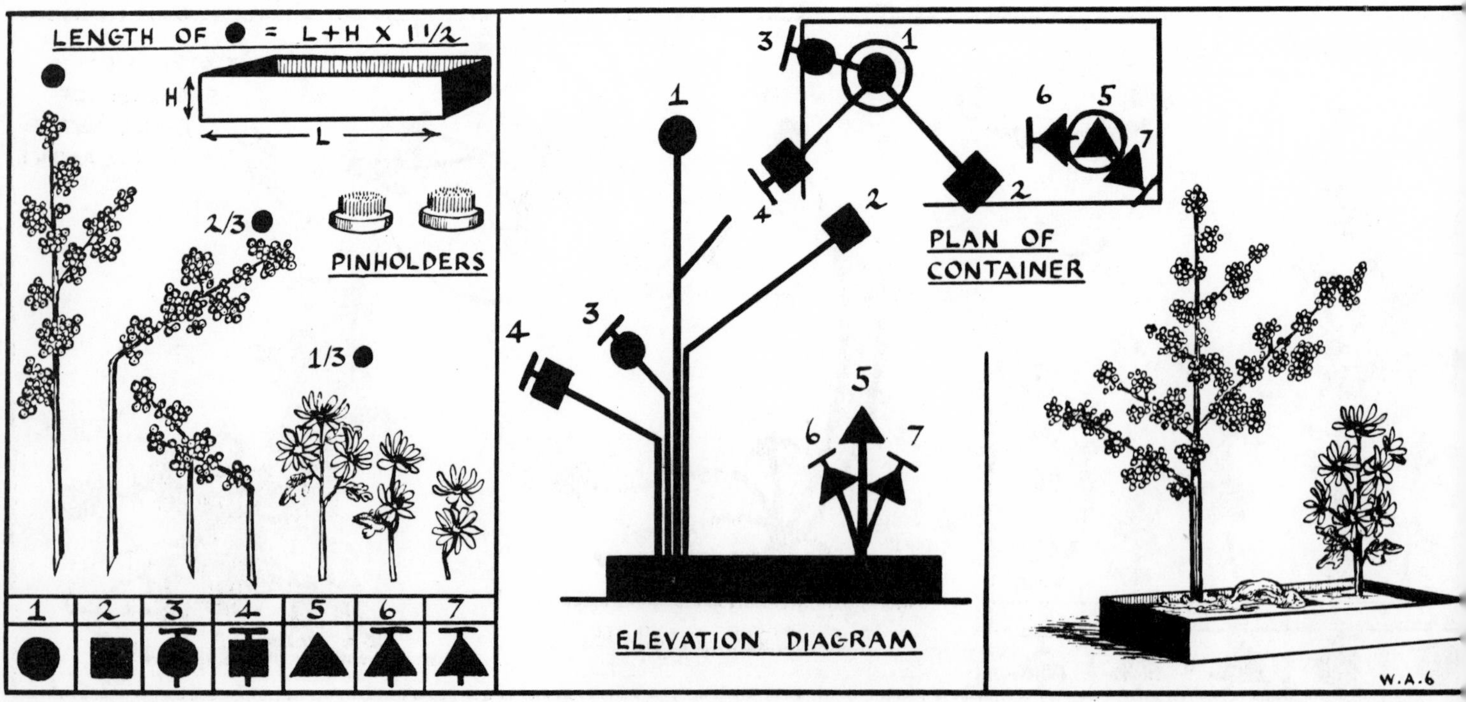

LENGTH OF ● = L+H X 1 1/2
H
L
2/3 ●
1/3 ●
PINHOLDERS
1 2 3 4 5 6 7
PLAN OF CONTAINER
ELEVATION DIAGRAM
W.A.6

# A Modern Style

FIVE PIECES OF EUPHORBIA, NINE CARNATIONS.

QUITE CLEARLY EACH OF THE COMPLICATED, THOUGH ATTRACTIVE, CONTAINERS REQUIRES A DESIGN OF ITS OWN.

A FEW RULES, SUCH AS THOSE OF MEASUREMENT, DO, OF COURSE, APPLY.

I HAVE USED ORANGE EUPHORBIA AND CARNATIONS THE COLOUR OF THE EYE OF THE EUPHORBIA

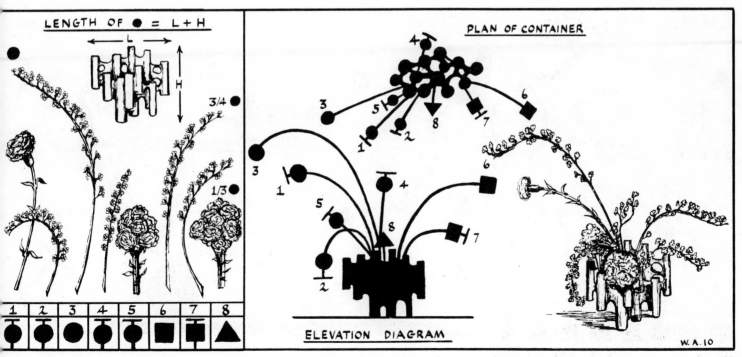

LENGTH OF ● = L + H

3/4 ●

1/3 ●

| 1 | 2 | 3 | 4 | 5 | 6 | 7 | 8 |

PLAN OF CONTAINER

ELEVATION DIAGRAM

W. A. 10

## A Natural Style

●, ◉, ■, ▣, ▲, ▲, ~ EIGHT ROSES IN ALL
"CAROL" IS LONG LASTING AND ONE
OF THE PRETTIEST OF SMALL ROSES ALTHOUGH
HER COLOUR COULD BE A LITTLE MORE SUBTLE.

TWO SMALL CONTAINERS ARE PLACED AT
ANGLES TO EACH OTHER. A SIMPLE FIXING IS
USED FOR ●, ■, ▲, ROSES.

SPECIAL CARE IS NEEDED TO SEE THAT
ALL SIDES OF THE ARRANGEMENT ARE EQUALLY
GOOD.

KEEP THE WATER TOPPED UP AND YOU
HAVE A TABLE DECORATION FOR WEEKS.

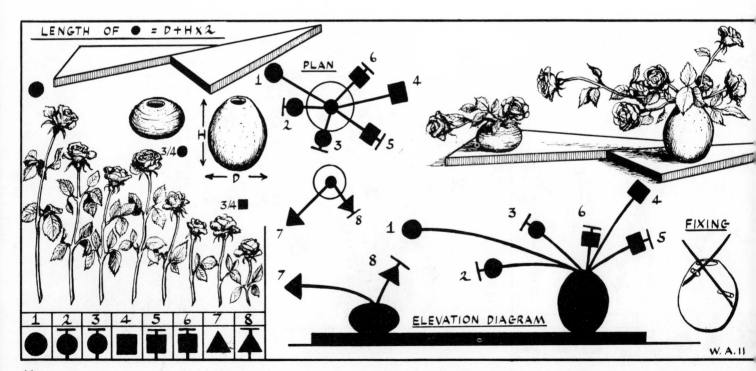

# A Natural Style

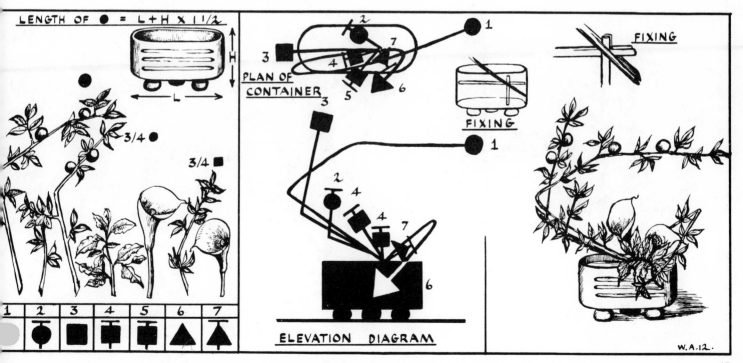

LENGTH OF ● = L + H × 1 1/2

PLAN OF CONTAINER

FIXING

FIXING

ELEVATION DIAGRAM

W.A.12.

| 1 | 2 | 3 | 4 | 5 | 6 | 7 |
|---|---|---|---|---|---|---|

# An Abstract

AN ABSTRACT RECLINING FIGURE

A PIECE OF TREE IVY HAVING BEEN SHAPED, TRIMMED AND SCRAPED WAS SMOOTHED WITH A FINE GLASS PAPER AND WAXED.

TWO FLOWERS MADE FROM NATURAL MATERIAL WERE ADDED AND THE WHOLE SENT TO THE GARDEN CLUB OF NEW JERSEY, U.S.A. FOR AN EXHIBITION

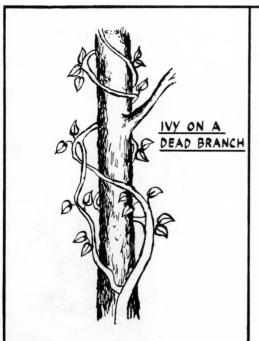

IVY ON A DEAD BRANCH

# WINTER

DRIFTWOOD, BARE OR EVERGREEN BRANCHES, LUMPS OF GLASS, SCRAPS OF METAL, CLASSICAL BRONZE, OR MODERN IRON CONTAINERS ARE THE COMPONENTS OF WINTER ARRANGEMENTS.

KEEP THE WATER LEVEL LOWER IN HIGH CONTAINERS AND MATERIALS TO THE FRONT TO OBVIATE THE CHILLY LOOK OF WATER IN THE LOW ONES.

CUT THE HARDWOOD BRANCHES AT AN ANGLE AND SPLIT THEM BEFORE IMPALING THEM ON A PINHOLDER.

TO KEEP DRIED BRANCHES IN POSITION USE THE PEG METHOD BEING CAREFUL TO FLATTEN THE SIDES THAT TOUCH.

HEAVIER WOOD IS EASIER TO MANAGE IF NAILED TO A FLAT WOODEN BASE. IN ALL YOUR WORK TRY TO ADHERE TO THE PRINCIPLE OF THE ASYMMETRICAL TRIANGLE.

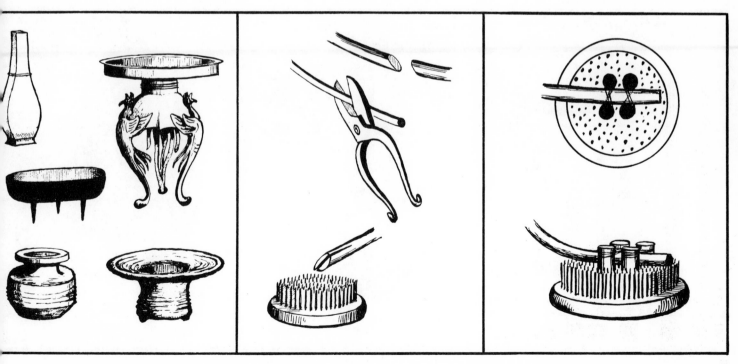

## A Free Style

FOR ●, ■, CURVE AND TIE THE THIN BRANCHES OF WEEPING WILLOW INTO LONG AND MEDIUM LOOPS.

▲ PINK ROSES PLACED BETWEEN THESE LOOPS.

USE SHORT GROUPS OF PINE TO COVER THE PINHOLDER AND FORM A BASE.

TIE THE LOOPS OF WILLOW FIRMLY. THE CONTAINER IS A CINNAMON BROWN COLOUR

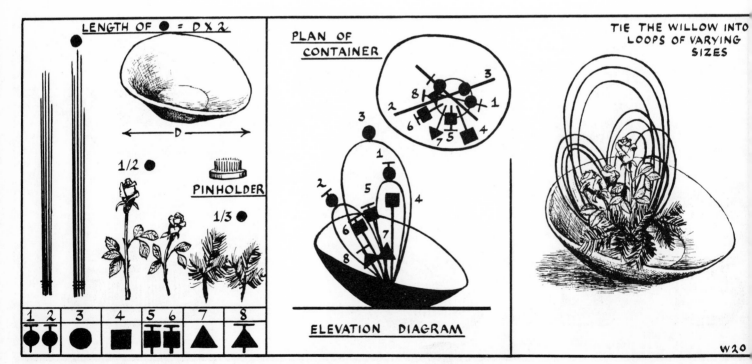

LENGTH OF ● = D X 2

1/2 ●

PINHOLDER

1/3 ●

| 1 | 2 | 3 | 4 | 5 | 6 | 7 | 8 |
|---|---|---|---|---|---|---|---|

PLAN OF CONTAINER

ELEVATION DIAGRAM

TIE THE WILLOW INTO LOOPS OF VARYING SIZES

W20

# A Modern Style

●, ⊤̇, ▲, ⊼̇, CALLA ( ARUM LILIES )

WHITE CALLA FLOWERS WITH EMERALD STEMS.

A TURQUOISE COLOURED CONTAINER.

TURN THE LILIES SO THAT EACH SHOWS A DIFFERENT FACET OF ITS BEAUTY.

IN THIS ARRANGEMENT THE INTERMEDIATE LINE ■ IS OMITTED.

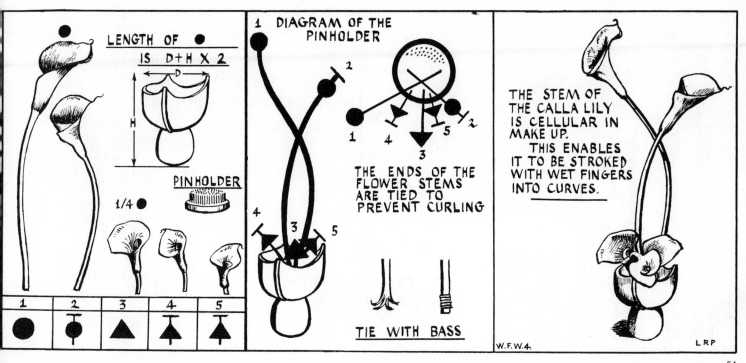

LENGTH OF ●
IS D+H X 2

PINHOLDER

1/4 ●

| 1 | 2 | 3 | 4 | 5 |
|---|---|---|---|---|
| ● | ⊤̇ | ▲ | ⊼̇ | ⊼̇ |

1 DIAGRAM OF THE PINHOLDER

THE ENDS OF THE FLOWER STEMS ARE TIED TO PREVENT CURLING

TIE WITH BASS

THE STEM OF THE CALLA LILY IS CELLULAR IN MAKE UP.
THIS ENABLES IT TO BE STROKED WITH WET FINGERS INTO CURVES.

W.F.W.4

LRP

51

## A Modern Style

● BLEACHED SUMMER CYPRESS, ■, LEAVES , ▲, CLIVIA

WHEN ●, ■, AND ▲ ARE OF DIFFERENT MATERIALS EXTRA CARE MUST BE TAKEN WITH THE CHOICE OF CONTAINER AND GENERAL COLOUR SCHEME.

MY CHOICE OF CLIVIA AS THE ▲ WAS TO HARMONISE THE CONTAINER AND BASE LINE, BOTH BEING OF RUST AND ORANGE HUES.

THE GREEN LEAVES OF ■ ARE USED AS A FOIL AND THE ● OF NATURAL COLOURED SUMMER CYPRESS IS CLIPPED TO EMPHASIZE THE INTERESTING SHAPE OF THE CONTAINER.

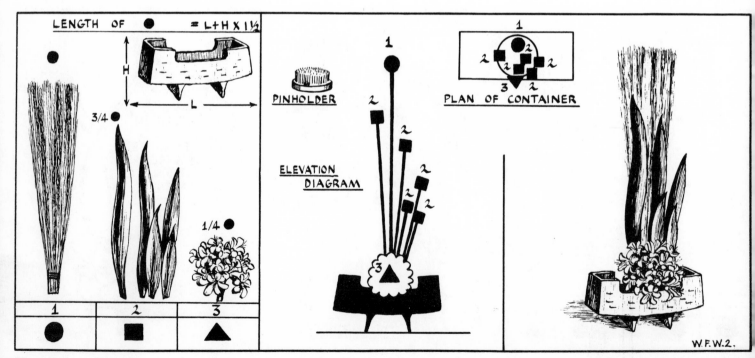

## A Free Style

●, ■, HAMAMELIS MOLLIS BRANCHES.
▲, ⧖, BUNCHED FREESIA.

THE RUSSET COLOURED BARK OF THESE BRANCHES IS ACCENTUATED BY THE RICH COLOURS OF THE FREESIAS, AS IS THE 'EYE' OF THE HAMAMELIS FLOWER.

A SALT GLAZE CONTAINER IN NATURAL BROWNS AND DEEP YELLOWS WITH MATT FINISH COMPLETES THE DESIGN.

THE ■ WAS CUT FROM THE TOP SECTION OF THE ●.

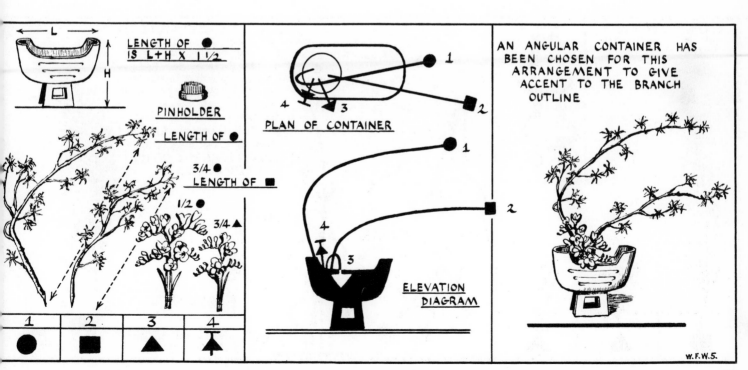

LENGTH OF ●
IS L+H X 1½

PINHOLDER

LENGTH OF ●

3/4 ● LENGTH OF ■

1/2 ●

3/4 ▲

| 1 | 2 | 3 | 4 |
|---|---|---|---|
| ● | ■ | ▲ | ⧖ |

PLAN OF CONTAINER

ELEVATION DIAGRAM

AN ANGULAR CONTAINER HAS BEEN CHOSEN FOR THIS ARRANGEMENT TO GIVE ACCENT TO THE BRANCH OUTLINE

W.F.W.5.

## A Free Style

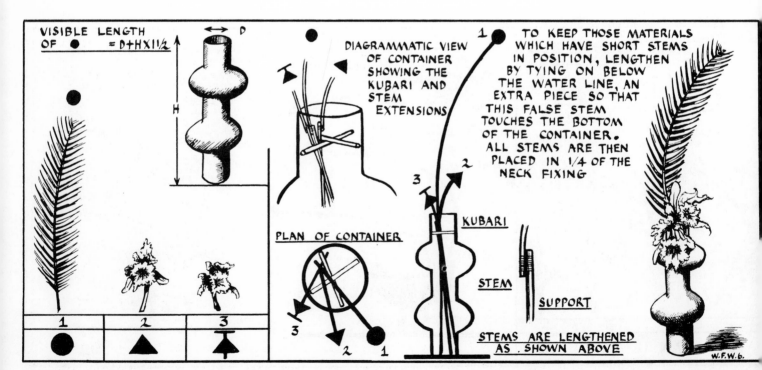

VISIBLE LENGTH
OF ● = D+H×1½

DIAGRAMMATIC VIEW
OF CONTAINER
SHOWING THE
KUBARI AND
STEM
EXTENSIONS

PLAN OF CONTAINER

TO KEEP THOSE MATERIALS
WHICH HAVE SHORT STEMS
IN POSITION, LENGTHEN
BY TYING ON BELOW
THE WATER LINE, AN
EXTRA PIECE SO THAT
THIS FALSE STEM
TOUCHES THE BOTTOM
OF THE CONTAINER.
ALL STEMS ARE THEN
PLACED IN 1/4 OF THE
NECK FIXING

KUBARI

STEM

SUPPORT

STEMS ARE LENGTHENED
AS SHOWN ABOVE

| 1 | 2 | 3 |
|---|---|---|
| ● | ▲ | ⊽ |

W.F.W.b.

54

# A Modern Style

IN THIS ARRANGEMENT ●, (D+H), TAKES THE FORM OF A MASS OF GREEN.

THE STEMS WITH LEAVES ARE TIED TO A CENTRE STICK AND TRIMMED TO FORM THE DESIRED SHAPE.

■ (3/4●), IS MADE FROM WHITE SPRAY CHRYSANTHEMUMS, TIED TO A CENTRE STEM FOR SUPPORT. MAKE SURE THAT ALL STEMS REACH THE WATER.

▲ (1/3●), IS OF GROUPED HOLLY BERRIES USED FOR CONTRAST IN COLOUR AND TEXTURE. BRING BASE OF ▲ FORWARD PARTIALLY TO MASK THE RIM OF THE CONTAINER.

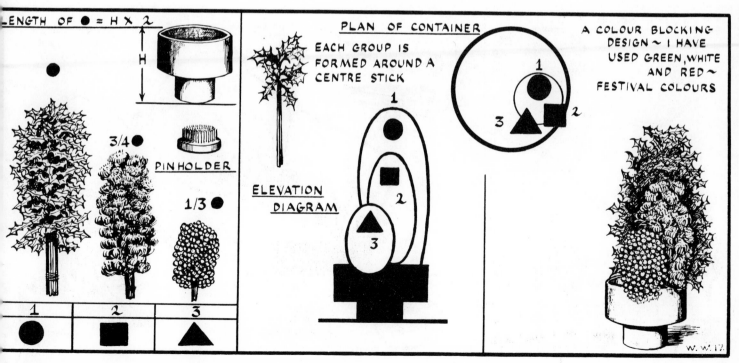

LENGTH OF ● = H X 2

H

3/4●

PINHOLDER

1/3●

| 1 | 2 | 3 |
|---|---|---|
| ● | ■ | ▲ |

EACH GROUP IS FORMED AROUND A CENTRE STICK

PLAN OF CONTAINER

ELEVATION DIAGRAM

A COLOUR BLOCKING DESIGN ~ I HAVE USED GREEN, WHITE AND RED ~ FESTIVAL COLOURS

W. W. 17.

## A Free Style

● WOOD, ●̄ ▲ CROTON LEAVES, ▲ PROTEA.
    THIS IS AN ARRANGEMENT IN WHICH A PIECE
OF DRIFTWOOD IS USED TO EMBELLISH A CONTAINER
AND CREATE INTEREST IN A SINGLE EXOTIC FLOWER.

    ▲ A PROTEA FLOWER OR ANOTHER EXOTIC
FLOWER OF SIMILAR SIZE. ∼ POPPY ∼ AMARYLLIS.
    ●̄ , ▲ , LEAVES OF THE CROTON PLANT OR LEAVES
TO ACCENT THE COLOUR OF THE FLOWER SUBSTITUTED.
    CAREFUL FIXING IS REQUIRED TO KEEP THE
DRIFTWOOD IN POSITION . WATERPROOFING OF THE
WOOD WILL PREVENT DISCOLOURATION.

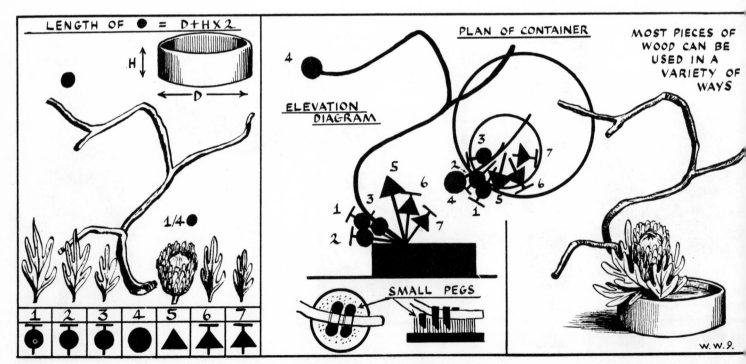

LENGTH OF ● = D+H×2

H

D

1/4 ●

| 1 | 2 | 3 | 4 | 5 | 6 | 7 |
|---|---|---|---|---|---|---|

ELEVATION DIAGRAM

4

5

6

3

1

2

7

PLAN OF CONTAINER

3

2

4

1

5

6

7

SMALL PEGS

MOST PIECES OF WOOD CAN BE USED IN A VARIETY OF WAYS

w.w.9.

## A Natural Style

●, ⊕, ▲, ♠, HOLLY BRANCHES, ⬤ POINSETTIAS.

IT WILL BE NOTED THAT IN THIS ARRANGEMENT NO ■ IS USED. THIS IS TO ALLOW PLENTY OF SPACE AROUND THE POINSETTIA FLOWERS TO SHOW THEIR BEAUTY.

IN SO LOW A BOWL OBSCURE THE PINHOLDER WITH PEBBLES AND A FEW SHORT PIECES OF HOLLY.

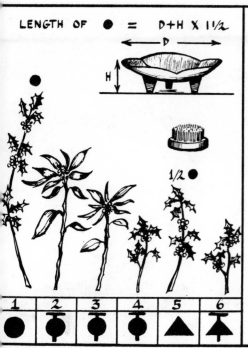

LENGTH OF ● = D+H X 1½

1/2 ●

| 1 | 2 | 3 | 4 | 5 | 6 |
|---|---|---|---|---|---|
| ● | ⊕ | ⊕ | ⊕ | ▲ | ♠ |

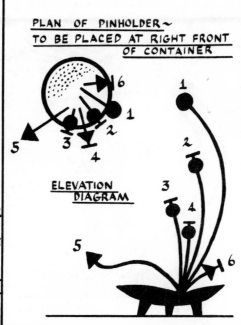

PLAN OF PINHOLDER ~
TO BE PLACED AT RIGHT FRONT OF CONTAINER

ELEVATION DIAGRAM

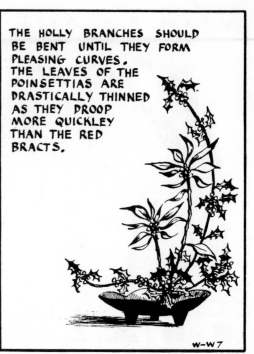

THE HOLLY BRANCHES SHOULD BE BENT UNTIL THEY FORM PLEASING CURVES. THE LEAVES OF THE POINSETTIAS ARE DRASTICALLY THINNED AS THEY DROOP MORE QUICKLEY THAN THE RED BRACTS.

W-W 7

## A Classical Style

A SWIFT SAILING BOAT

●, ■, ▲, T, ALL OF STRELITZIA LEAVES
▲ A STRELITZIA FLOWER

THE ● AND ■ ARE CURVED TO GIVE THE
IMPRESSION OF A FULL SAIL IN STRONG WIND.
THE STREAMER LIES JUST ABOVE
THE SURFACE OF THE WATER ~ THE WAKE.

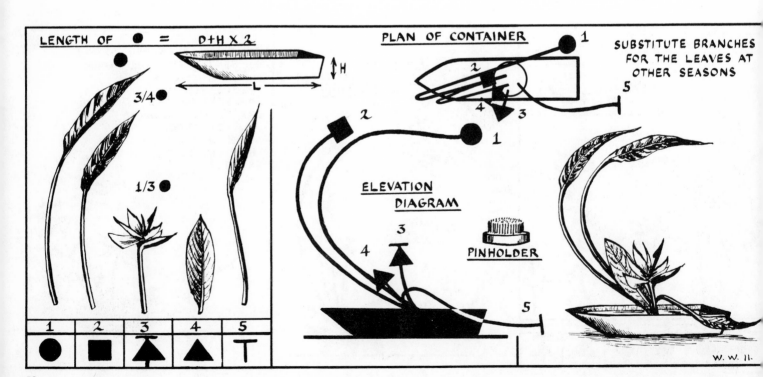

LENGTH OF ● = D+H X 2

PLAN OF CONTAINER

SUBSTITUTE BRANCHES FOR THE LEAVES AT OTHER SEASONS

3/4 ●

1/3 ●

ELEVATION DIAGRAM

PINHOLDER

| 1 | 2 | 3 | 4 | 5 |
|---|---|---|---|---|
| ● | ■ | ▲ | ▲ | T |

W. W. II.

## Classical Style

THE QUINTESSENCE OF IKEBANA

●, ■, ▲, THE ASPIDISTRA LEAF

A STUDENT STARTS WITH THE SELECTION OF LEAVES BY SIZE AND TYPE.

TYPE A ~ NARROW SIDE TO THE LEFT.

TYPE B ~ NARROW SIDE TO THE RIGHT.

THE BALANCING OF THE POSITIVE (WIDE) AND NEGATIVE (NARROW) SIDES IS IMPORTANT FOR THE STUDENT OF A CLASSICAL SCHOOL.

THE THREE LEAF ARRANGEMENT REQUIRES ● ~ A ■ ~ B, AND ▲ ~ B. THESE ARE CURLED, TIED LOOSELY AND PLACED IN DEEP WATER BEFORE BEING ARRANGED.

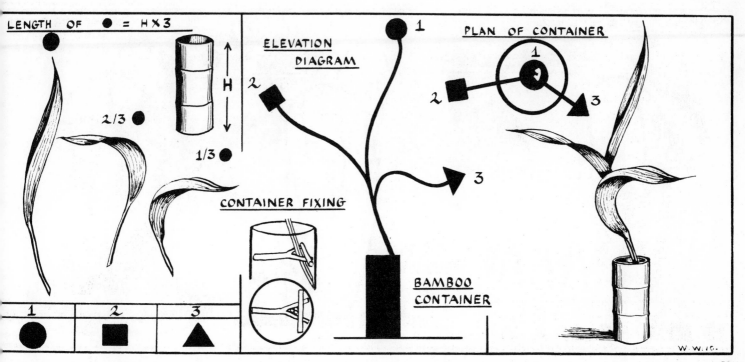

LENGTH OF ● = H × 3

2/3 ●

1/3 ●

H

ELEVATION DIAGRAM

PLAN OF CONTAINER

CONTAINER FIXING

BAMBOO CONTAINER

| 1 | 2 | 3 |
|---|---|---|
| ● | ■ | ▲ |

W. W. 10.

## A Free Style

A FESTIVAL STYLE WILLOW AND TINSEL.

●, ■, WEEPING WILLOW CAREFULLY CHOSEN FOR LINE.
▲, THREE WISE MEN, OR ANGELS, OR ANY CHRISTMAS GROUP.
　　TINSEL~THIS IS LOOSELY WOUND AT THE BASE AND
PROGRESSIVELY CLOSER AS THE TIPS ARE REACHED.
　　COVER THE BASE (AND PINHOLDER) WITH COTTON
WOOL WHICH HAS BEEN 'FLUFFED' BY WARMING AND
LIGHTLY SPRINKLED WITH GLITTER.
　　THE HIKAE FIGURES MAY BE MADE SIMPLY WITH
A BAUBLE, A SEMI-CIRCLE OF STIFF COLOURED PAPER
AND A SMALL PIECE OF PAPER SHAPED AS A CROWN.

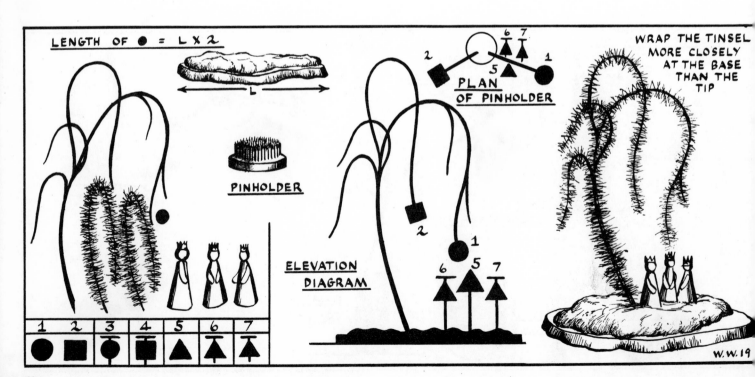

LENGTH OF ● = L X 2

PINHOLDER

PLAN OF PINHOLDER

ELEVATION DIAGRAM

WRAP THE TINSEL MORE CLOSELY AT THE BASE THAN THE TIP

W.W. 19

| 1 | 2 | 3 | 4 | 5 | 6 | 7 |